Love

Compassion

Caring

Heart

Healing

Acceptance

Harmony

Anahata

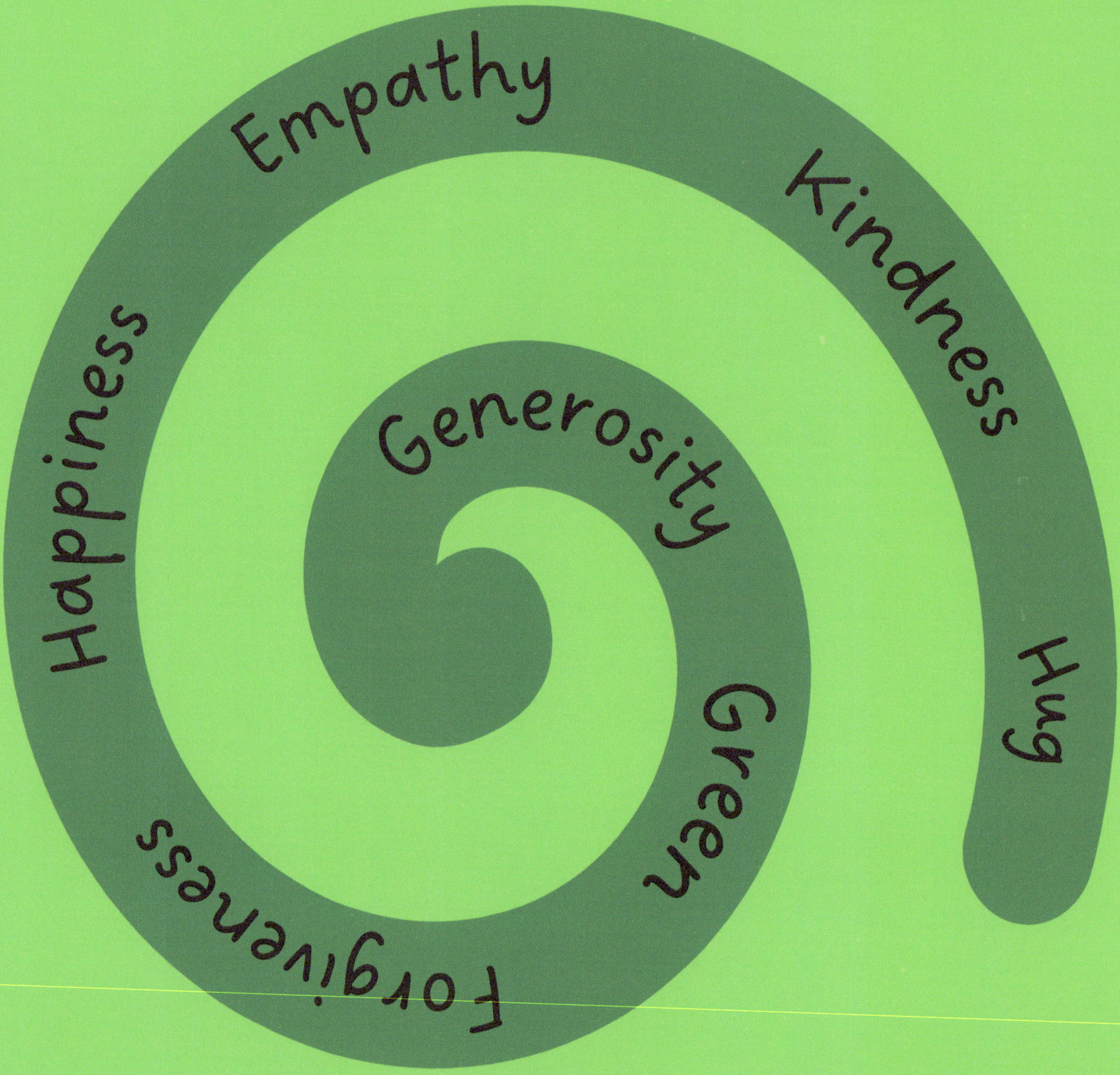
Empathy
Kindness
Hug
Happiness
Generosity
Green
Forgiveness

Heart Chakra Adventures:

Embracing Love
with
Emerald and Green

Volume 4

By: K.C. Gold

"This book is dedicated to you.
Seek out new experiences with an open heart."

Northern Lights Publishing LLC.

https://northernlightskids.com/

Hello, I'm Emerald,
And next to me is Green,
We're spinning energy particles,
Where love is seen.

They call us Heart Chakra,
Where love's the guide,
Nestled within your chest,
Is where we reside.

We're the energy force
Igniting gratitude so bright,
Allowing you to bask in
Beauty and joyous light.

We love to have fun
And help you too,
But sometimes we need a
hand,
It's true.

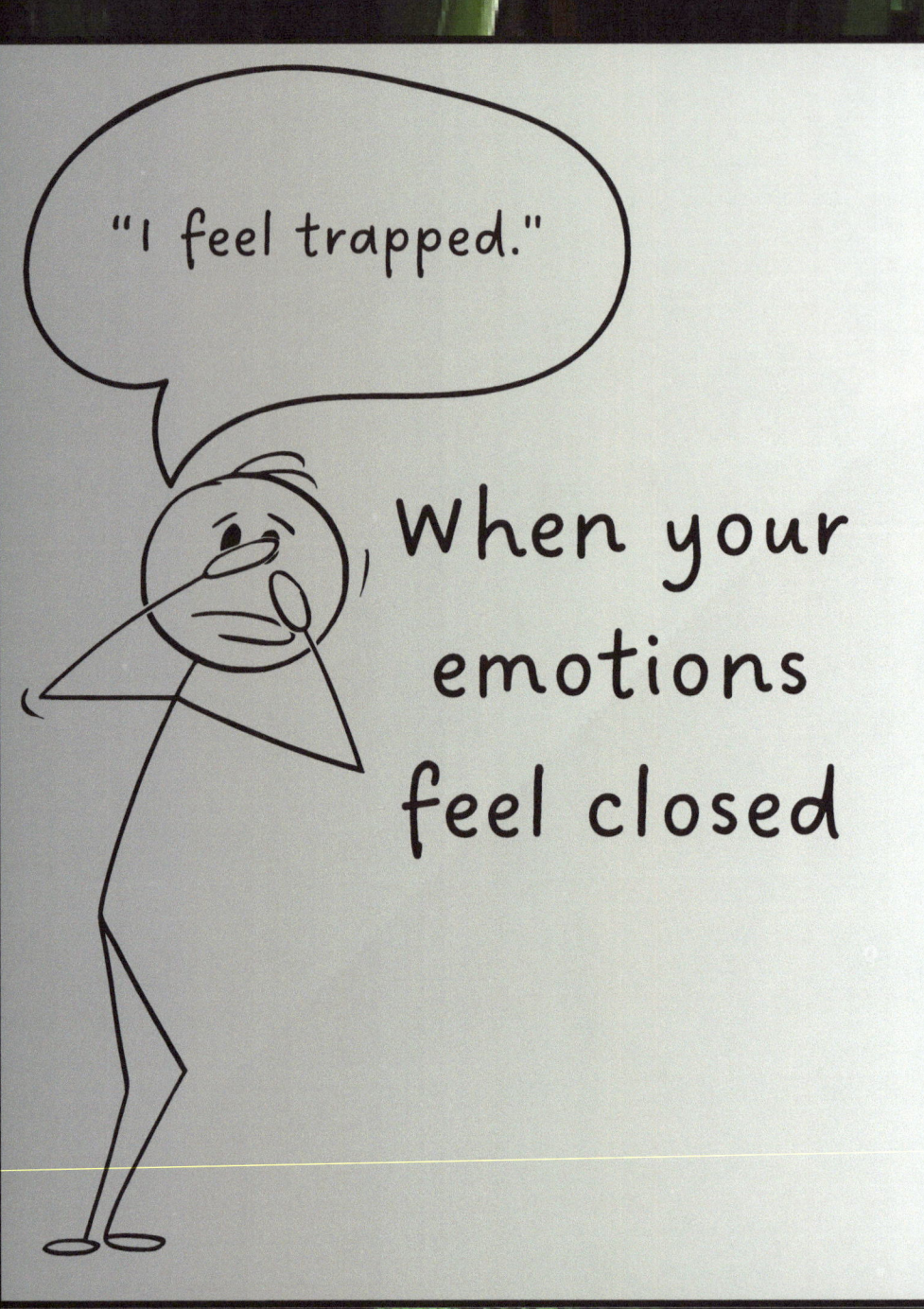

And
making a
connection
takes a fight,

Our spin slows down,
And starts to lose its light.

There's much you can do
To set us in a whirl,
And get us spinning back
around again,
639 times then curl.

Hertz Meter

1 Hertz (Hz) = 1 Spin Per Second

639Hz

'F' is our favorite tone,
Its sound a sweet delight,
Hearing it our spin ignites
Soaring to new heights.

Dance and move your body,
Feel the rhythm's sound.

Eat something green,
That grows from the
ground.

Dress in the color green
Until you feel serene,
And when you do, our spin
will move,
Filling you with glee.

Do whatever you need,
We're here, it's true,
Fully supporting you,
In all you do.

Sit in a quiet place,
Pick a mantra that feels
right.
After you repeat it,
You will start to feel just
right.

"Inside my heart,
A spark so bright,
The power of love
Shining its light."

"Love's my compass,
Guiding my way,
Spreading kindness
and joy every day."

"Past behind me,
Future ahead,
With love in my heart,
I forge ahead."

"Out with the old,
In with the new,
Making space for love
To breakthrough."

In the emerald embrace,
Feel your spirit rise,
As we guide you through the
stars,
Into the skies.

Emerald and Green,
Dancing in the glow,
Waking up your Heart
Chakra,
Letting love flow.

With kindness and care,
Let your heart's light shine,
Heart Chakra embrace,
Pure and divine!

Love Compassion Heart Harmony Acceptance Healing Caring Anahata

Dear Reader,

Thank you for taking the time to read this book. If you found value in it, I would be incredibly grateful if you could take a few moments to leave a review. Your feedback not only helps me improve but also aids other readers in discovering books they might enjoy.

Thank you once again for your support and for being a part of this adventure!

Warm regards,
K.C. Gold

Amazon

Northern Lights
Publishing

Seek out new experiences with an open heart.

www.ingramcontent.com/pod-product-compliance
Lightning Source LLC
Chambersburg PA
CBHW041433120626
46547CB00002B/197